TEN
CATHOLICS
Lives to Remember

Kenneth Christopher

Winston Press, Inc.
430 Oak Grove
Minneapolis, MN 55403

Other books in the series:
Prayer: A Discovery of Life
Jesus of Nazareth: A Life Worth Living

Design and Production Services: Canning Mulvehill Productions, Inc.
Design: Kathleen Weflen
Cover Photograph: Louis Ferreri
Project Directors: John Kirvan and Roger Radley

Library of Congress Catalog Card Number: 82-51242
ISBN: 0-86683-715-9

5 4 3 2 1

Winston Press, Inc.
430 Oak Grove
Minneapolis, MN 55403

Preface

This book may make it seem as if the story of the Catholic Church in the United States can be summed up in the lives of a few heroic individuals. In fact, just the opposite is true. If one could tell the story of Catholicism in America it would have to be told through the lives of simple people—thousands of them, millions of them—most of them poor and hardworking. They came from countries like Germany, Poland, Ireland, or Italy to make a living for themselves in the new world, and most of them succeeded. They were not heroes, except in the ordinary sense that most people who lead good lives are heroes.

Because the Catholic Church in the United States was composed largely of poor, simple people, American-style Catholicism had unique flavor. The Church in Europe was often associated with wealthy and powerful groups of people. As a result, Church institutions there tended to support the rich. When the oppressed poor rose up in revolt to overthrow their governments (as they did in France), the Church also suffered. In the United States, however, the Church and the poor people stood side-by-side against persecution and economic oppression.

This helps to explain why certain "heroes" in this book spent so much of their energies caring for the poor. Dorothy Day and Rose Hawthorne Lathrop were directly engaged in ministering to poor people in large cities. Terence Powderly helped to organize workers into unions. Bishop John Hughes was an early civil rights leader for the poor immigrants who poured into America's cities. These people served the poor because it was their Christian duty; but they also did it because they *were* the poor.

In our own day Catholics in America are no longer the poorest group in society—except for Spanish-speaking Catholics who are still oppressed and persecuted. It remains to be seen whether American Catholics will remember their roots and continue to reach out to less-fortunate brothers and sisters. That is one reason this book was written: to help us remember where our roots are.

All of the events in this book actually happened. However a few of the dialogues—like that between Charles Carroll and his father—were partly invented to give the stories more drama. Most of the quotes attributed to different people were things they actually said or wrote.

The author would like to thank John Kirvan, who first suggested this book. He would also like to thank his wife Pat and his sons Chris and Kenny for their patience during the writing. All of these people are part of my roots, and I can't forget them.

Contents

Charles Carroll Becomes the First Citizen

The year is 1773. The place is Annapolis, the small, wealthy seaport city that serves as the capital of Maryland colony.

Two men are standing in a richly furnished room of a private mansion. The older man is larger, with a red face and a loud, irritated voice. The younger man is slimmer and quieter. Despite the differences in their bodies, their features are remarkably alike. In fact they are father and son—both of them named Charles Carroll.

"Blast it, I don't like it, Charles," says the older man, clutching a newspaper in an angry fist. "Did you see what the *Maryland Gazette* is printing? A story defending the governor, that's what! The man is a tyrant and a dictator. He defies the laws made by our legislature and yet this newspaper writer defends him. What do you think of that?"

The younger Charles Carroll takes the newspaper from his father and calmly spreads it out on a polished table in front of the fireplace.

"I saw it. It was an interesting article," the younger man says with a smile. "Who do you think wrote it?"

"Dulany, of course. The colonial secretary. He's a clever lawyer and an ally of the governor."

"I agree with you," says the younger. "He's so

1

clever he doen't even sign his name. Look at this. He writes a dialogue between two make-believe citizens. The first citizen is critical of the governor; then the second citizen makes a fool of the first one by pointing out the errors of his arguments. Very smart."

The older man shakes his head ruefully. "He's probably the smartest lawyer in the colony. Everyone is afraid to tangle with him. What we need is another lawyer who is just as smart as he is to take him on."

"Who could that be, Father?"

The elder Charles Carroll frowns, deep in thought. "Well…maybe *you*, Charles."

His son bursts into laughter. "You can't be serious, Father. Remember, I'm not allowed to practice law in this colony. Good heavens, they won't even let me vote!"

The two men look at each other for a long moment of silence. Then the the father places his arm affectionately across his son's shoulders and sighs.

"I know, son," he says quietly. "I know what it's like. We'll just have to find someone else."

Charles Carroll, father and son, were members of one of Maryland's oldest and most prominent families. The older man's father, also named Charles Carroll (which makes three Charles Carrolls in a row), first came to Maryland in 1688 as private secretary to Lord Baltimore, who ruled Maryland with permission of the King of England. The first Charles Carroll became attorney general and one of the leaders of the colony.

The arrangement in Maryland worked well because Carroll, Lord Baltimore, and the King of England were all Catholics. In those days of bitter religious warfare, a king protected persons who belonged to his Church but persecuted members of other Churches.

Then William III, a Protestant, became the new King of England and things changed in Maryland. Charles Carroll lost his job as attorney general and, in fact, was put in jail for a short time. New laws forbade Catholics to hold any public office. Catholics could not vote in elections, nor could they have their own churches and schools.

The idea that each person should be free to worship God in his or her own way was not recognized in the 17th and 18th centuries. In England Catholic priests were hunted down and jailed or expelled from the country. The same thing happened to Protestant ministers in Spain, where Catholics were in control. Jews were persecuted everywhere.

Each side believed all the others were wrong. And since they also believed that "people in error have no rights," they felt it was proper to deny others their civil rights, such as the right to worship openly, to practice certain professions, or take part in politics.

For the Carroll family, this meant that they had no friends in the government. Charles Carroll— the former attorney general—and his son — Charles Carroll of Annapolis—became businessmen and traders instead of government leaders. Because they were good at their jobs, they soon became one of the richest families in Maryland. By the time the third Charles Carroll was born they were, perhaps, the wealthiest family in America.

The youngest Carroll went to school in France with his cousin Jackie. Charles trained to be a lawyer, and Jackie studied to be a priest. But when he came home Charles couldn't practice law, because that was one of the forbidden professions for Catholics. So he went into the family business.

He got married and raised several children in a big house near the city. To keep people from getting him mixed up with his father who had the same name, he called himself Charles Carroll of Carrollton.

One thing about the Carrolls: They had no love for the English king or other leaders who used their power unfairly. They knew what it was like to be pushed around.

The father and son who talked by the fireplace in Annapolis were upset because the royal governor in Maryland made decisions contrary to the wishes of the elected assembly.

"He's a dictator, that's what he is," said Charles Carroll the father. "But who will stop him? No one wants to tangle with this fellow Dulany."

"Don't worry, Father," said his son. "Maybe I can think of someone."

The next week the *Maryland Gazette* carried another account of a debate between the "First Citizen" who supported the people's side and the "Second Citizen" who defended the governor. Except this time the best arguments were made by the "First Citizen."

Soon all the people in Annapolis were talking

about it. Who had written the most recent article? Surely not Dulany. Who, then? Who was smart enough and had the legal training to argue with the great Dulany? Slowly their attention turned to young Charles Carroll of Carrollton—the man everyone tended to ignore because he was a Catholic.

Suddenly Carroll was a celebrity. As he rode down the street, pale and slim on his fine horse, people would turn and whisper, "There he is. He's the one who wrote the 'First Citizen' letters."

Women smiled at him and men tipped their hats. Even those who disagreed with him were impressed with his learning and good manners.

Everyone, that is, except Daniel Dulany. The famous lawyer was angry.

The next week a new letter was printed in the newspaper bitterly attacking the "First Citizen." Calmly Carroll replied to it the following week. Neither man used his real name, but everyone knew it was Dulany against Carroll.

By this time all of Maryland was following the newspaper debate. Dulany attacked, Carroll answered—and answered well—defending the rights of the people against the governor. No matter what Dulany wrote, Carroll outdid him. Finally, seeing that he couldn't win the political argument, Dulany went after Carroll's religion.

Asked Dulany, "Who is this man who calls himself a citizen and attacks the governor and the governor's council?"

Answering his own question, Dulany went on: "He has no share in the legislature, as a member of any branch. He is incapable of being a member. He is disabled from having a vote in the choice of representatives by the laws of the country—on account of his principles which are distrusted by those laws."

And to make his point very clear, Dulany concluded, "He is not a Protestant."

So there it was. The hate and suspicion of old religious wars were being carried into American politics. Dulany was counting on the hope that Marylanders would share his own prejudices.

What Dulany didn't realize was that times were changing. Even as he wrote those words, men like Thomas Jefferson and John Adams were dreaming of a new nation where people would be free. And that freedom would have to include freedom of religion—the right of citizens to belong to whatever Church they chose.

Could Catholics be good citizens? Could they give allegiance to the state as well as to the Church? Not even Jefferson and Adams knew the answer to that, but they knew they had to take a chance that the answer would be yes.

That was the situation when Carroll picked up his pen to answer Dulany. As always, his response was calm.

"To what purpose are these threats being made against me?" Carroll asked Dulany in his next letter. "Why am I told that my conduct is not in keeping with my membership in society?"

The purpose, Carroll intimated, was to muddy the political debate by inflaming old religious hatreds.

The position of Catholics in Maryland was very delicate, Carroll went on. Their existence was tolerated, but not their participation in public affairs. Dulany's kind of prejudice threatened their very existence.

"The government allows me to live here. But if you, sir, rouse popular resentment against Catholics through mean and wicked statements, thus leading to their persecution, we will soon see whether the government supports toleration or not."

The real point of Carroll's reply to Dulany was unspoken: If it was wrong to solve political disputes by stirring up religious hatred (and on this the public solidly supported Carroll), it was equally wrong to bar Catholics from public life in the first place.

The new United States must have complete religious toleration or none at all.

In this famous exchange of letters, Carroll emerged as the clear winner. A few days after the last letter appeared, Maryland held an election for its colonial legislature. The patriot party that opposed the governor won a landslide victory. The new legislators marched through the streets of Annapolis to the home of Charles Carroll and publicly thanked him for his help.

The man who couldn't even serve in the legislature because he was a Catholic was, indeed, the "First Citizen" of Maryland.

The Dulany episode was the beginning of a new career for Charles Carroll of Carrollton.

Three years later he was chosen to represent Maryland at the Continental Congress in Philadelphia, and there he became the only Catholic to sign the Declaration of Independence.

With Benjamin Franklin, Carroll visited Canada in an effort to convince settlers there to support the American Revolution. Another member of the Canadian expedition was Carroll's cousin Jackie, now called John, who by this time had been ordained a priest. John Carroll later became the first American citizen to be consecrated a bishop, and he lived to become Archbishop of Baltimore and the most influential Catholic churchman in America.

The Canadian trip did not meet with success, but Carroll and Franklin became lifelong friends.

Charles Carroll was a member of the state legislature in Maryland for many years, and he served one term in the United States Senate. He continued to be active in the business world, being one of the founders of the Baltimore & Ohio Railroad.

In his last years he was a greatly revered figure. He lived to be 95 years old, making him by far the oldest living signer of the Declaration of Independence. People would come from miles to see the "Old Signer"—a frail, dignified man who still rode his horse through the streets of Baltimore. The gentle Charles Carroll of Carrollton turned out to be much tougher than anybody thought he would be.

Joseph Machebeuf Finds a Ruin, and a Treasure

He came across it in the late afternoon, after a day of riding across the baking hot Sonora Desert, his horse and the horses of his two Mexican riders covered with dust. They could see the building for a long time before they reached it. It stood white against the pale blue sky and purple hills that surrounded the town of Tucson.

"There is the mission," one of the riders said.

"It's beautiful," said the priest, almost in awe. "But it's all by itself, in the middle of nowhere. Why in heaven's name did they build a church way out here?"

"It's not nowhere," said the first rider. "It's Arizona."

The church building was larger than anything the priest had seen north of Mexico. Of course there had been grander churches back in France where he grew up, but the other church buildings in the American Southwest were simple, one-room structures of adobe—mud bricks that often seemed ready to fall down, and sometimes did. This was a tall, strong mission church, built in the Spanish style with curling lines, a dome, and sturdy towers on each side of the front door. There was a walled churchyard, and behind it another building, probably a rectory.

The priest was Joseph Machebeuf (pronounced mosh-berf). He had been sent by his bishop in Santa Fe to explore this new mission country extending for thousands of miles across the arid wasteland of New Mexico and Arizona. He and his companions had been on the trail for weeks, eating corn meal and occasional game and sleeping under the stars, always alert for Indian attacks. Their trip took them into Mexico to find the bishop who once ministered to Catholics in this territory and to have him transfer authority to the American bishop.

Now they were back in the United States, riding toward the ancient mission church of San Xavier del Bac which had been built 150 years earlier by Jesuit missionaries. But the Jesuits and the Franciscans had been gone for decades. No priests lived here now.

As they came close, they could see the church was nearly a ruin. The roof was potted with holes and the outer walls were flaked and crumbling. A few Indian women and children ran for cover as the men dismounted.

"Papagos," said Machebeuf's guide, naming the tribe of Indians.

"They look poor enough—just like this church," said the priest. "It's a shame! This must have been a beautiful building once."

They went inside. The afternoon sunlight reflected dimly from the white adobe walls. Looking toward the front of the church, the priest gasped in surprise. The church was beautiful still. Rich gilt pillars adorned the sanctuary. Fresco paintings of Jesus and Mary decorated the walls, and on either side of the bare altar stood wooden

10

statues painted in bright colors that glimmered through layers of collected dust.

Machebeuf looked at it for a long time. No other church in New Mexico or Arizona was as fine as this. And here it was decaying, deserted, uncared for.

But not quite deserted. A shadow moved off to one side.

"*Hola! Madre!*" one of the riders called.

A woman came toward them out of the gloom. An Indian woman. She approached slowly, not knowing what to expect.

"What are you doing here?" the rider asked in Spanish.

"Praying," she said shyly. She was looking at Machebeuf, the white man.

"You were praying?" Machebeuf asked in amazement. "But there is no sacrament here, no priest."

"It is still our church," said the woman. "We pray here. Sometimes we sing."

A smile broke slowly over Machebeuf's face. I am a priest, " he said. "I have come to bring Jesus Christ to you once more, and to this church."

Joseph Machebeuf was born in southern France on August 12, 1812. His father was the leading baker in the village of Riom. As a young man Joseph decided he wanted to be a priest, and so he entered the seminary at Clermont. He was ordained in 1836.

While still a student, Machebeuf had become close friends with another seminarian, John Baptist Lamy (pronounced la-mee), two years younger than himself. Machebeuf was short, dark, excitable, and a constant talker. Lamy was a tall, gentle, quiet man. They balanced each other perfectly.

The two young men had often talked about becoming missionaries after their ordinations. Already many French priests were working in the cities and forests of America. Bishop Benedict Flaget of Bardstown, Kentucky, was French-born, as was Bishop Simon Bruté of Vincennes, Illinois. Because of the way the Catholic Church was persecuted during the French Revolution, many French priests fled to the new United States, and then liked it so much that they stayed.

Shortly after Lamy's ordination the two priests accepted the invitation of Bishop John Purcell of Cincinnati to become missionaries in that diocese. They left home without telling anyone because they feared their families would object. After a voyage of forty-three days across the Atlantic Ocean, their ship arrived in New York.

For eleven years Machebeuf and Lamy served as pastors in the rough and growing settlements of northern Ohio. They built churches with their own hands and traveled by horseback and carriage for weeks at a time caring for their scattered parishioners.

Then, in 1850, Lamy was named bishop of the new Diocese of Sante Fe in the New Mexico Territory—land that had just become part of the United States as a result of the Mexican War. Lamy demanded that his old friend Machebeuf accompany him, and so the two set out on an adventure greater than either of them had ever expected.

If the Ohio experience was difficult, New Mexico was nearly impossible. Merely getting there required a journey by wagon caravan that took weeks, all the time threatened by violent storms and hostile Indians.

The new diocese was larger than all of France. It was a land of deserts, rugged mountains, raging rivers, and few roads. There were sixty-six church buildings in the diocese, but only twelve priests to tend them—and several of the Spanish-speaking priests soon departed because they resented the Americans taking over.

Machebeuf's energy and good nature were tested often in the next few years. It was a hard life. There were not enough people to do the work or enough money to do it with. Machebeuf spent long months on the trail visiting lonely villages in which lived people who had not seen a priest in years.

One day, approaching a solitary ranch, he discovered the building was under attack by fierce Apache Indians. The rancher and his terrified family were huddled inside. Seeing Machebeuf coming near, the Indian band rode toward him threateningly. Their leader challenged Machebeuf.

"Are you with the army?" asked the chief in Spanish.

"Not with the army," said Machebeuf. He drew out his crucifix and showed it to the chief.

"Are you a priest?"

"Yes, a priest."

"Good," said the chief. "Welcome." He shook hands with Machebeuf and had each of his followers shake hands with him too. When the greetings were finished, the chief had another question. Had Machebeuf seen any soldiers in his travels?

"Certainly," said Machebeuf. "I passed some this morning. They are coming along right behind me."

After a short discussion among themselves, the Indians declared they had to leave. They galloped away, and the relieved ranch family thanked Machebeuf for his quick thinking.

Quick thinking, however, could not by itself bring comfort to the people of the New Mexico Territory who hungered for the presence of God. Without enough priests or churches or schools, they had to make do with what they had. When a priest came by—that was a time for celebration.

Standing in the ruined church of San Xavier del Bac, Machebeuf was joyously welcomed by the Indian woman he had found praying. She ran ahead to tell her family that a priest had returned to the mission. The Papagos insisted he sit down for a meal. While he ate, they sang one of the hymns they remembered from long ago.

Machebeuf was touched. "Imagine that," he said. "After all these years they still remember. They still pray and sing."

Later on he had an even greater surprise. One of the village elders motioned for Machebeuf to follow him. He led the way into a poor dwelling where he produced a rolled-up Indian blanket. He unrolled it on the floor. Inside were four silver chalices, a gold-plated monstrance, two golden cruets for holding water and wine, a pair of silver candlesticks, and other treasures.

Machebeuf was amazed. "I don't understand," he said. "Where did these come from?"

"The church," replied the old Indian. "We hide them so that no one will steal them. We know a priest will come back someday.

"Take them. Stay with us," the Indian said.

"I will use them," Machebeuf said, "and then I will give them back. For I cannot stay. Keep them safe. They are your treasures. Someday a priest will come who will be able to stay. Then your church will be rebuilt like new, and these sacred cups will be used to give honor and praise to God."

For a few weeks Machebeuf remained, serving the Catholic population at the mission and in neighboring Tucson. For a short time San Xavier del Bac was a church where Mass was celebrated and sermons preached. Without a bell to call the people, Machebeuf borrowed an army cannon that he fired to announce the beginning of services. Americans, Mexicans, and Indians flocked to him.

But at last it was time to go. Missionaries in that country had to keep moving. Machebeuf sadly noted that the church still needed repairs. Perhaps another priest would come to live there. Someday.

As he rode away with his two companions, Machebeuf looked back at the old mission.

"You make them happy, *Padre*," said the first rider. "You bring God to them."

Machebeuf sighed. "No," he said, "perhaps I bring God a little closer. But God was there already. Those people already possess a great treasure."

Father Joseph Machebeuf labored as a priest and missionary in the Diocese of Santa Fe for eighteen years. For the last eight of those years he was assigned by his old friend Lamy to the Colorado region where gold had been discovered, bringing a new stream of miners and settlers from the East.

Instead of hot deserts, Machebeuf had to get used to snow and steep mountain roads. One particular road was too dangerous. His carriage fell from a narrow ledge to some rocks below. His leg was badly injured. He never was able to ride a horse again, and he walked with a limp for the rest of his life.

In 1868 Machebeuf was named as the first bishop of a new diocesan territory that included Colorado and Utah. He served in that position until his death in 1889.

Just three years earlier he had celebrated the 50th anniversary of his ordination as a priest. One of the tributes that came to him at that time declared that "from the Gulf of California to the Mississippi Valley the name of Machebeuf is known."

By the time of Machebeuf's death priests had come back to stay at the old mission church of San Xavier del Bac. Gradually the church was repaired and its bells once more rang out across the Sonora Desert. It still stands today in full splendor a few miles south of the city of Tucson.

Bishop Hughes
Battles the Nativists

In 1847 the country of Ireland was struck by a great natural calamity. It was not an earthquake or a flood. It was a blight that infected the country's potato crop, leaving millions of tons of potatoes rotting in the ground. Not only the farmers suffered as a result; all the Irish suffered, because potatoes were a crucial source of food for the Irish people. Much of the population faced the immediate threat of starvation.

What do people do when they are hungry and without food? They move someplace where food is available. For the Irish in the 1840s and 1850s that meant the United States.

The Irish had been emigrating to the United States before the "potato famine," of course. In the ten years prior to 1840 more than 200,000 Irish came to America. In the decade of the potato famine, however, 780,000 Irish made the trip to America, and in the next decade nearly a million more came over. Add that to the million Germans who came over during the same decade and you have immigration on a grand scale.

For the first wave of Irish in the 1830s and 1840s, America meant freedom as well as food and jobs. Ireland was not an independent nation in those days. England ruled Ireland, and ruled it strictly. It was fair to say that the Catholic Irish and Protestant English did not like each other. Naturally the Irish were happy to escape from

English Protestant control. In America, they told themselves, there was no state Church and people were free to worship God however they chose. The Bill of Rights guaranteed it.

So the Irish traveled to the United States and settled into eastern cities like Boston, New York, and Philadelphia. They found jobs and sent their children to the free public schools. And their children brought home their schoolbooks and their parents discovered...what?

The parents discovered that the schoolbooks and the schools themselves were really Protestant books and Protestant schools.

The proud Irish Catholic parents had been tricked! The schools weren't "public" schools at all. They were Protestant denominational schools operated with public money. The books used in the schools weren't merely Protestant; they were filled with references of hatred directed toward Catholics—warning about the dangers of "popish practices," about evil priests and wicked nuns. One geography book used in New York elementary schools at this time declared;

> *Superstition prevails not only at Rome but in all the states of the Church. The inhabitants observe scrupulously all the ceremonies of religion, although apparently destitute of true devotion.*

Christians of a later era might just laugh at such ignorance. Relations between Catholics and Protestants in our day are warm and friendly. A century ago, however, religious differences were deadly serious. Hatreds that grew out of religious wars in Europe were still fresh in people's minds.

What were the Irish parents in New York going to do? They were not well enough organized to elect a new government that would change the schoolbooks. They were too poor to afford their own system of parochial schools. Instead the children were simply taken out of the public schools and left to wander through the streets. As many as 20,000 Catholic children in New York City attended no school at all.

Clearly something had to be done about it.

Just about this time John J. Hughes was appointed bishop of the Catholic Diocese of New York at the time. Bishop Hughes was a strong-willed and combative clergyman who was never known to avoid a fight, especially when it involved his beloved Irish.

Hughes was born in Ireland in 1797 and emigrated to the United States with his family when he was nineteen years old. The family settled in Maryland. Hughes studied for the priesthood at Emmitsburg, Maryland, and was ordained for the Diocese of Philadelphia.

The young priest gave evidence of a belligerent character early in his career. He was confronted by a group of laity who tried to get control of one of Philadelphia's Catholic parishes. Hughes helped to crush them, as he would crush all attempts by nonclerics to have a voice in the Church from then on. He also involved himself in an acrimonious debate with a Presbyterian minister over the merits of their two Churches. The debate embarrassed believers on both sides, even though Hughes enjoyed it immensely.

Hughes became bishop of New York in 1839,

succeeding Bishop John Dubois (pronounced du-bwa), a French-born cleric. Dubois had been a gentle and kindly administrator of the diocese—much too polite to press for any radical change. Hughes was made of different stuff.

The opening gun in the battle against the New York school system was actually fired by Governor William Seward, who suggested hopefully that some money might be made available to instruct the Irish "by teachers professing the same faith."

Hughes immediately leaped on the idea, demanding a "just proportion" of the state money available for education. Those who ran the public schools offered to compromise and change the textbooks to make them acceptable to Catholics. But Hughes wanted more than that; he wanted state money for Catholic schools.

Hughes took his petition before the New York City Common Council where for two days arguments were heard. It was a wild and raucous confrontation between Hughes and a number of Protestant clergymen and school officials. They traded insults, argued about Church history, and sometimes even talked about education. In the end Hughes warned; "Either the consciences of Catholics must be crushed or the public school system must be destroyed."

The Common Council ruled against Hughes and his followers. Undaunted, the bishop turned to the state legislature, asking it to replace the private agency that ran the city's "public" schools. At a meeting of Catholics in the city, Hughes promised that help was on the way. "There is but one course for you to take," he said. "Stand up for yourselves and public men will soon come to your aid."

It quickly became clear that Hughes knew which public men he wanted. He proposed a list of candidates for election to the legislature, all of them being men who would support the Catholics. His opponents were angry and upset. It wasn't considered proper then (or now) for clergymen to tell citizens which candidates to vote for. One newspaper that opposed Hughes warned that "The foot of the beast [that is to say, the Catholic Church] was trampling on the elective franchise, and its high priest was standing before the ballot box, dictating to his obedient followers the ticket they must vote…"

Hughes didn't care what they said. As it turned out, his list of candidates was elected, the legislature passed the laws that he wanted, and soon the school system of New York City was reorganized, giving Catholics as much influence as Protestants had.

Three days after the law was approved a crowd of angry rioters marched on the bishop's residence. Bricks crashed through the windows and the doors were knocked in before police arrived to restore order. It proved that religion and politics generated a lot of feeling in 1842

In his long tenure as bishop and later archbishop of New York, John Hughes functioned as a civil rights leader as much as a religious leader. His battle with the New York public schools had little to do with religion. It was really concerned with the rights of Catholics to equal protection under the law.

Many Protestant Americans were genuinely afraid of Catholics a hundred years ago. They were afraid that the millions of Catholics emigrating to this country would eventually take over the government and perhaps weaken the Protestant religion. "The tide is constantly swelling and breaking over us," lamented one public official. "We cannot repel it now even if we wanted to." There were others, however, who felt that the Catholic influence should be repelled, and they were willing to try anything to do it.

This anti-Catholic movement was called "Nativism" because it pitted the natives (Yankee Protestants) against the newcomers (ethnic Catholics). The hostility between the two groups over minor issues was often violent. In 1844 a Nativist mob in Philadelphia went charging through the Catholic neighborhoods of that city, burning and looting two churches and a convent. Many people were killed during the three days of rioting.

There were rumors that the rioters were heading for New York City. John Hughes was ready. He announced to New York public officials that "if a single Catholic church is burned in New York, the city will become a second Moscow"— alluding to the way French soldiers had destroyed that Russian city.

"Are you afraid some of your churches will be burned?" he was asked.

"No, sir," the bishop answered. "But I am afraid some of *yours* will be burned. We can protect our own. I come to warn you for your own good."

The bishop's warning had its effect. Not a single Catholic church was touched.

If Hughes' methods sound blunt and sometimes crude, it ought to be remembered that he lived in an era when public politeness was not highly regarded. Nativist newspapers regularly spoke of Hughes in venomous terms. The bishop responded in kind. He once described a United States senator as "a sincere, honest, and—as far as the two ideas can be associated—honorable bigot."

The surprising thing is that in spite of the constant parade of public disputes that marked his career, Hughes gradually earned the admiration, or at least respect, of nearly everyone. Presidents invited him to Washington for conversations. President Lincoln even sent him on a mission to Europe to explain the Union side of the Civil War. Toward the end of his life *Harper's Weekly* described him as a "self-made man" who "awes into silence any serious opposition." The magazine added that "no individual, perhaps, in this country, in office or out of it, wields a larger influence over a greater number of minds…"

That description was true of Archbishop Hughes even in the last months of his life. In the summer of 1863 throngs of poor Irish in New York City gathered to protest the drafting of soldiers for the Civil War. The protest quickly became a riot, and for several days the city was the scene of open warfare between Irish-Americans and government troops. Scores of people died. Finally Hughes helped to calm the tempers of rioters by pulling himself from his sickbed and speaking to 5000 people from the window of his residence. He talked to them, he blessed them, he told them to go home, and they did. So the fighting bishop helped in the end to bring peace to his city.

John Hughes was by far America's most influential Catholic churchman in the 19th century. He was a colorful battler at a time when the Church needed a battler to protect it and insure its growth.

But like many heroes he was born for his own particular time; he would not fit comfortably into our time. His belligerent attitude toward Protestants, for instance, would be unsuitable in today's climate of interchurch friendship.

Even the causes he championed had some unhappy side effects from our point of view. His insistence that the Church be directed only by priests and bishops tended to put lay people in a silent and subordinate place. It has taken lay people until now to reclaim their role as equal members of the Christian community.

His battle over the New York City public schools also had some bad long-term effects. By ridding the school system of its Protestant influence he unintentionally contributed to the movement to exclude religion from every aspect of public life— so that now children are legally forbidden to pray or read the Bible in public schools. Because Catholics and Protestants couldn't decide a hundred years ago which religion was going to dominate, religion was removed from public life and became a private affair.

These were not results that Bishop Hughes wished; they were just things that happened. Hughes did what he had to do. Today, if you go into St. Patrick's Cathedral on New York's Fifth Avenue, it's nice to remember that Bishop John Hughes laid its cornerstone. The things he built far outnumber the mistakes he made.

Mrs. Lathrop Moves from One Nice Family to Another

Scammel Street was nearly empty in the winter twilight, its unplowed center lane heavy with crusted, dirty snow. A bitter wind was whipping off the East River and down the length of the street so that the few people who dared to come out had to lean against it for balance while using one free hand to hold down their hats.

Usually the street was filled with noise and people. Even on cold nights those who lived in the dingy walk-up apartments liked to gather on the street where they could socialize and move around to keep warm. It was better than being inside. None of the crumbling tenements had toilets or hot water, and few of the residents could afford enough firewood to keep them warm.

But on this night no one went outside who didn't have to. It was too cold.

A woman in a long, heavy skirt picked her way along the icy track that passed for a sidewalk. She wore a wide-brimmed hat with a dark veil that completely covered her face. Holding the veil in place with one fist, she occasionally looked up at the house numbers as if searching for the right building.

At last she stopped in front of 1 Scammel Street, next door to a stable. It was a building no better than any other on the block. Maybe worse.

The woman went up three steps and in the door. The unlit lobby was dusky in the twilight. It smelled of coal smoke, stale food, and unwashed people. The woman leaned against the wall to gather her strength, then began going up the crumbling staircase.

On the second floor were several closed doors, but one of them was different. The others were dark and grimy. This one had a fresh coat of shining white paint. And in the center was a cast-iron knocker.

After a moment's hesitation she reached for the knocker and let it fall once. She heard footsteps inside. The door opened to reveal a room as white and fresh as the door. The woman holding the door wore a clean, gray dress. Her tawny red hair was done up with pins, and her hands, although rough from soap and hard work, were delicate and tapered. A gentlewoman, no doubt about it. The woman with the hat felt awkward and embarrassed.

"Excuse me, ma'am. Someone gave me your name and said you could help me. I don't mean to be no bother."

The woman holding the door looked back at her with steady eyes. "What seems to be the problem?" she said. Her voice was rich and musical with an accent the visitor couldn't place for sure. Maybe Boston.

"They said you were a nurse and that you could take care of my bandage," said the visitor. She lifted the veil to show a bandage that covered her nose and one eye.

"I can't get anyone else to do it. Unless I get some help they'll send me to the Island."

The woman's voice quavered. Blackwell's Island was the last stop. That's where the poor were sent to die.

The woman in the apartment opened the door wider.

"Come in," she said.

Inside, the apartment was clean but simple. A few wooden boxes served as stools. The fireplace was used for cooking as well as for warmth. There was a table against one wall holding bandages and ointments. On the wall were pictures of saints that the woman couldn't identify, although she knew they were saints. In the corner was a statue of the Blessed Mother.

"I'm Mrs. Lathrop," said the woman who lived there. "And you are…?"

"Margaret," said the visitor.

"Take off your hat, Margaret, and sit down. I'll be glad to help you if I can. But first I have to know if you have any money?"

"Oh, no, ma'am, but I'll try to pay you as soon as I get some," Margaret exclaimed. "I promise!"

"That's not necessary," said Mrs. Lathrop with a sudden smile. "If you had money you could go to the hospital. I only help those who can't pay. Now let's look at your bandage."

The woman named Margaret sat on one of the boxes while Mrs. Lathrop began to unwrap the gauze from her face. She waited, half expecting Mrs. Lathrop to back away when the bandage fell to reveal a hideous open wound. Most of her nose and part of one cheek were missing due to the spreading cancer.

"There!" said Mrs. Lathrop brightly. "We'll clean that out and put a nice, fresh bandage on."

Margaret sat there in wonderment. "You mean," she said in a small voice, "that you'll change my bandage and I don't have to pay you anything?"

"Yes," said Mrs. Lathrop. "Not only today, but in three days I'll change it again—and every three days after that. I'll give you an appointment."

Margaret was silent. She couldn't understand this woman who was willing to care for her disease that frightened other people away and who did it only on the condition that she wasn't paid.

"Excuse me, ma'am," she said at last. "Why do you do this for me? You're a lady, I can see that. Why would someone who comes from a nice family do this kind of work?"

Mrs. Lathrop straightened from her bandaging and brushed a wisp of hair from her forehead with the back of her hand.

"I *do* come from a nice family," she said reflectively. "A very nice family. But then"—her eyes meeting Margaret's, she smiled again—"both of us are in the same family, Margaret, God's family. That's why we have to help each other."

Mrs. Lathrop did come from a nice family. She was born Rose Hawthorne in 1851, the youngest child of Nathaniel Hawthorne, author of *The Scarlet Letter, The House of Seven Gables,* and many other stories still read and loved more than a hundred years later.

Rose and her family lived in Concord, Massachusetts, which was then the most famous literary town in America. Henry David Thoreau was her father's best friend. Ralph Waldo Emerson often dropped by for tea. Louisa May Alcott, who later wrote *Little Women,* lived next door to the Hawthornes and played with Rose when they were girls.

When Rose was still young, her family lived in Europe for a few years. Her father had accepted a government job in Liverpool, England. When that was finished, they spent several months in Rome where the Puritan Hawthornes were deeply affected by Catholic art and liturgy.

One day Rose was running through the garden behind the Vatican palace and actually collided with Pope Pius IX taking his afternoon walk. The surprised Pope excused her. He also gave her his blessing.

Some of his readers believed Nathaniel Hawthorne was a Catholic at heart. His stories often had to do with sin and repentance, and he was fascinated with the Catholic practice of confession. Yet, despite the attraction, he never became a Catholic officially. He died in 1864, still a Protestant, one day before Rose's thirteenth birthday.

By the time she was twenty her mother was dead too and Rose had married George Lathrop, a young New Yorker.

The Lathrop's marriage was not especially happy. Their only child died in infancy. George Lathrop was a writer and editor for the *Atlantic Monthly* in Boston and several newspapers in New York. But he drank too much liquor, which led to arguments and eventually to a separation from Rose.

In the meantime the Lathrops had undertaken a different kind of journey. In 1891 they were both received into the Catholic Church, thus completing what Rose's father had pointed toward.

With her marriage finally broken down, Rose looked for something to do. In years past she had dabbled in writing, publishing a few stories and poems, but that wasn't the kind of work she wanted now.

One day she took some clothes that needed mending to a seamstress who had done work for her in the past. She was told that the poor woman had become ill and had been taken off to Blackwell's Island because her disease was incurable. The woman died there in squalor and poverty.

Rose was shocked—and even more shocked when she visited Blackwell's Island herself. Couldn't something be done for these people, she wondered? Just because they couldn't be cured, did that mean their last days had to be so awful?

All at once Rose discovered the job she had to do. She was not a doctor or a nurse, but she was determined to save poor people who might otherwise die alone and forgotten. With only a short training period in a hospital, she set out for the city's slums.

It is hard today to appreciate the situation of wealthy, aristocratic Americans who converted to the Catholic Church in the 19th century. The Church was largely an immigrant church, composed of uneducated people, some of them unable to speak English. How does an educated convert fit into such a Church?

The story is told of a cultured Boston woman who became a Catholic and suddenly realized she had no one to tell; none of her Protestant friends would understand. So she looked up an old Irish laundress who used to work for her family, flew into the woman's arms and cried, "Oh, Mary, we are Catholics!"

After becoming Catholic, some converts tried to stay apart from the "immigrant church" they found in America. Orestes Brownson, the Unitarian minister from Boston, was one of those. He accepted the truth of Catholicism, but he was never truly comfortable in the Catholic community. Even Isaac Hecker, the convert who founded the Paulist Fathers, didn't mix intimately with the poor.

Rose Hawthorne Lathrop was another kind of person altogether. She threw herself vigorously into the service of the poorest and neediest immigrants. She lived in the slums, caring for people who were disfigured and dying. In their last days she would invite them into her apartment where they could die with dignity and love.

The woman called Margaret who came to Rose Lathrop on a winter night was like many other patients. She suffered from cancer—an ugly disease that had no cure. Margaret's relatives believed mistakenly that cancer was contagious. They didn't want to touch her bandages. They shrank from the open wounds on her face.

Mrs. Lathrop didn't shrink from them. Every few days Margaret returned to have her sores washed and her bandages changed. Because of the attention she received, her spirits picked up. She felt loved again. Sometimes she stayed to talk to Mrs. Lathrop.

"What I don't understand, ma'am, is why a fine lady like you is living in this neighborhood taking care of the sick," Margaret said one day.

Mrs. Lathrop paused in her work to look out at a ferry crossing the East River before replying.

"I don't believe there was anyone who loved fancywork, or reading novels, or painting, or going to the theater, or chatting socially with friends more than I did," she said wistfully.

"I remember the moment I realized I wouldn't be able to do all those things and still be faithful to the work heaven was giving me. I said, 'Oh, God, I can't make that sacrifice for you.' All the same, I knew I should make it."

"You did it because you're a good woman," Margaret said.

"Many women are good, including yourself, Margaret," Mrs. Lathrop answered.

"Wealthy women are not bad women," she continued. "Good—very good—people fulfill their social duties, make their houses look charming, embroider linen dainties for their tables, varnish the truth, and succeed in keeping themselves and their friends well and happy, until God sends sickness, shipwreck, or fire into their lives.

"There is an old story that comes to all of us in time. It is not a pretty story. It is a story of crime, famine, and forgotten souls. No matter how selfish we are we have to hear that story and respond generously. The work we can do then is much more absorbing than china painting or boat races. And when we do respond generously, we discover that what is hardest to do is the sweetest to see done."

It would be comforting to report that with the care she received Margaret recovered from her disease, but cancer in those days was incurable.

Margaret died, but she died surrounded by love and care.

What was the hardest to do was also the sweetest to receive.

Rose Hawthorne Lathrop continued to live in the slums, ministering to other cancer victims. After the death of her husband in 1898 (with Rose at his side), she found an order of Dominican sisters that devoted itself to the care of persons with incurable illnesses.

Mrs. Lathrop took the name of Mother Alphonsa, and she gave another thirty years of her life to establishing homes for the sick, training sisters, and promoting the cause of God's poor. She died at the motherhouse in Hawthorne, New York, in 1926. Her life—so hard in the living—was sweet to see lived.

Terence Powderly
Wins Two Victories

February, 1885. A wintery blast from the Great Plains swept through the darkened yards of the Wabash Railroad in Emporia, Kansas. A dozen men huddled around a fire they had built beside the tracks, their figures lurid in the ocher firelight.

These tracks were part of the Missouri-Pacific system, and the Missouri-Pacific was owned by Jay Gould. At that very moment, while a dozen men tried to keep warm in Kansas, Jay Gould was preparing to go to bed in his elegant New York townhouse, surrounded by all the luxury a person could wish for. He was a handsome man with a high forehead and fine whiskers. The newspapers called him a "robber baron," alluding to his reckless drive for money and power.

Fifteen years earlier Gould and Jim Fisk had nearly destroyed the American financial system when they tried secretly to corner the gold market and thereby control the price of gold. That venture failed, but it destroyed many honest businesses in the process. Now Gould by himself had decided to squeeze some extra profit out of his railroads. Workers on the Wabash were notified that their wages would be cut by 5 percent, and this came on top of a 10 percent pay cut levied only a few months earlier.

Then, all along the Wabash line, a strange thing happened. Men began to walk out of their jobs.

Engineers and crewmen put down their tools and walked away.

They said they were on strike.

It was a spontaneous thing. There were no votes. There was no press conference announcing the strike. Men just stopped working. Within a few days the strike spread to other Gould-owned lines: the Missiouri-Pacific, the Missouri, Kansas & Texas. Before the week was out there were 10,000 miles of railroad shut down by striking men.

The men in the Emporia yards were part of this movement. If you asked them, they would have told you they were members of the Knights of Labor, an organization that sounded more romantic than it really was. There were only about 105,000 members of the Knights of Labor from coast to coast. They included garment cutters in Philadelphia, telegraph operators in Denver, and spinners in Fall River, Massachusetts. Compared to Jay Gould and the other robber barons they were more like serfs than knights.

The men who stood around the fire in Emporia realized they were weak. But they were fired by an idea—the belief that if laboring people stuck together they could achieve a better way of life for the poor, unorganized, uneducated workers in the United States.

Would they succeed? Sometimes great issues are decided by very small events. On this night a single locomotive chugged and clanked from the engine house and into the yards where the strikers were keeping vigil. It approached them slowly. Powerless to stop the engine by force, the strikers moved aside. But as it passed one of the strikers called out, "For the sake of your family and ours, don't take that engine out!"

The engineer's name is not known, but his heart must have been touched. A hundred yards down the track the locomotive came to a halt. The engineer let all the steam out of his boiler and stepped down from his cab to join the group by the fire.

The strike was going to work.

There's one thing you should understand about labor unions a hundred years ago: it was dangerous for people to belong to them. Workers lost their jobs, and sometimes their lives, when they tried to organize against companies.

Industry leaders believed they had the permission of God and the United States government to make as much money as they could, even if other people got hurt in the process. And people did get hurt. Men and women worked twelve and fifteen hours a day in unsafe conditions for pitifully low wages. Children worked too. (As late as 1900, almost 20 percent of American children—some of them only ten and twelve years old—had full-time jobs.) If any of these people dared to strike, they were met by gun-toting guards hired by the shop owners.

When workers and management argued, it frequently led to violence. A few years earlier some Pennsylvania miners known as the Molly Maguires waged guerrilla warfare against the owners of the coal mines. A number of the Molly Maguire chiefs were caught and hanged.

When the Noble and Holy Order of the Knights of Labor was founded in 1869, its leaders decided that it would be safer for the members if their names were kept secret. Before they were allowed to join, prospective members were asked, "Do you believe in God, the Creator and Father of all? Do you obey the Universal Ordinances of God, in gaining your bread by the sweat of your brow? Are you willing to take a solemn vow binding you to secrecy, obedience, and mutual assistance?"

Only after they said yes to this were the workers allowed to undergo the secret ceremony of admission to the union.

The growth of the Knights was slow. Many people were afraid to join. And because of the secrecy it was hard to find someone who would admit to being a Knight or to discover where a local meeting was being held.

Finally—and this was the strangest of all—the growth of the Knights was held down because of opposition within the Catholic Church. A large percentage of American workingmen were Catholic immigrants, and so the disapproval of the Church discouraged people from joining.

Churchmen were suspicious of the Knights because with all of its talk about solemn vows, secrecy, and obedience the union was like an underground church. In years past the Church had suffered at the hands of Masons and other secret societies in Europe. In addition, many bishops and priests believed in their hearts that God should be on the side of progress, by which they meant the factory, the railroad, and the mine.

Faced with the violent hostility of business owners, the indifference of the government, and the suspicion of the Church, the Knights of Labor needed effective and adroit leadership.

38

Leadership. That was the key. Traditionally labor leaders have been gruff, burly men—former coal miners, steamfitters, iron workers—plainspoken, forceful, and uncomplicated. The leader of the Knights of Labor was Terence V. Powderly, who didn't fit the pattern at all. Powderly was a dapper Pennsylvanian with an elegant handlebar moustache and pince-nez eyeglasses.

Powderly didn't like to travel. He preferred to stay home in Scranton, whose citizens had three times elected him as their mayor. He didn't like going to union gatherings because the men drank beer, and Powderly hated alcohol in all forms. And Powderly was one union leader who didn't like strikes. He called them "a relic of barbarism." This is the man, then, who had to stand up to Jay Gould and battle for the strikers of the Wabash Railroad.

Yet in Powderly was a streak of something tougher and more determined than his outer looks indicated. Powderly was a battler.

"I stand on the side of God's poor, alongside those for whom Christ died," he once declared. And it was largely true. Powderly stood with the common people against the bankers, business leaders, and (sad to say) many churchmen.

His strongest supporter in the Catholic hierarchy was Cardinal James Gibbons of Baltimore. Even as the Wabash strikers were marching in the winter of 1885, Gibbons was preparing to support the Knights among the American bishops—and in Rome, if need be. Gibbons saw clearly that it would be a disaster for the Church if the Vatican condemned the Knights and thereby lost the allegiance of the American working people.

Would the Catholic Church condemn the Knights of Labor? Would Jay Gould win the struggle of the Wabash Railroad? Through the winter of 1885 the answers to these questions hung in the balance.

Although he was opposed to strikes in principle, Terence Powderly worked mightily to make this strike succeed. The union had two main demands—the restoration of the wage scales that had existed before Jay Gould cut everyone's pay and the rehiring of all the men who went on strike.

Gould resisted, but what could he do? His railroad was shut down. Public sympathy was with the strikers. The governors of Missouri and Kansas were urging him to agree to the union demands. Finally Gould could take it no longer. He broke down and accepted the conditions set by the Knights of Labor. It was victory for the strikers!

The settlement of the Missouri-Pacific Railroad strike in 1885 was the first big victory for American labor unions. Terence Powderly and the Knights of Labor had done something no one had ever done before. By standing together they had beaten the robber barons of industry.

After the strike it didn't seem so dangerous to be a union member. In fact so many people wanted to join the Knights of Labor that within one year the membership jumped from 105,000 to 703,000.

And another, perhaps bigger, victory was being won in Rome. With arguments supplied to him by Powderly, Cardinal Gibbons managed to stop the Vatican from condemning the Knights as some other, more conservative, prelates had wanted.

Not only did Pope Leo XIII not condemn the Knights, but in 1891 he issued an encyclical *Rerum Novarum* that supported the right of working people to form unions and strike. The Catholic Church had taken a stand that has been reaffirmed by Popes and councils ever since: The Church would stand behind the little people, the poor and oppressed, the workers and the tradesmen. And in America that meant that the working people would remain Catholic instead of dropping out of the Church as many workers had done in Europe. Catholics would continue to play central roles in the leadership of American labor unions for another century.

The success of the Knights of Labor was short-lived, however. Terence Powderly and the other leaders of the Knights were too gentle for the new age of unionism that was dawning in America. The new, aggressive American Federation of Labor gradually took membership away from the Knights. Powderly quit as its leader in 1893 and not long after that was appointed to a government job by President McKinley. He worked in the United States Bureau of Immigration until 1921, three years before his death.

Even as a government employee Powderly never stopped being a champion of the poor and the working classes. Once, late in his life, someone called him an "agitator." Powderly did not deny it. In fact he was proud of it.

"During all the years I was General Master Workman of the Knights of Labor," he wrote, "I had a picture above my desk representing Jesus Christ, the world's greatest, most sublime agitator, he whose heart, moved by indignation and pity, condemned the wrongs inflicted on the toiling poor by the rich and powerful.

"Didn't they call him an agitator when they said, 'He stirs up the people'? Didn't he pay the penalty for being an agitator when they pressed the thorns into his flesh and nailed his hands and feet to the cross? Christ, if I read him right, did not die for the unjust rich man any more than he died for the lazy poor man. He lived and worked for the industrious poor, for them he agitated, for them he died."

Terence Powderly devoted his life to those people too.

Al Smith Leads, But the Nation Doesn't Follow

The reporters stood in a huddle just inside the door of the 69th Regimental Armory on New York City's Lexington Avenue. For a while they had been kept outside the huge red brick building, but because of the November cold they had been allowed to come in. They stood in a group— about thirty of them—ready to pull out their notepads in case anybody of importance came by.

Somewhere inside the building members of the Tammany Society were gathered waiting for the election returns. Waiting with them was the candidate, the man who would find out that night whether or not he would be the next president of the United States.

Several reporters were leaning over a radio in an adjutant's office. Thanks to the miracle of radio the winner of the election might actually be known that very evening. In years past it often took days to add up and announce all the votes. But this was the modern era. This was 1928.

An hour went by. The news on the radio was not favorable for the candidate. There was a buzz of amazement when several Southern states— states that usually voted for the Democratic candidate—showed early strength for the Republican, Herbert Hoover. Even New York was swinging to Hoover.

Eventually the newsmen were reduced to astonished whispers. It looked like a landslide, a humiliating defeat for the man who waited inside. He was being overwhelmed by Hoover.

Before long there was a bustle of activity in the corridor. The candidate was coming out. Newsmen bustled and bumped each other for the best positions.

"Governor! Governor Smith! What do you think of the election returns?"

The candidate was standing in the doorway. He was a moderately tall man dressed in a topcoat and a floppy-brimmed hat. He had a strong Irish face with a large nose and sensitive mouth. His right hand held a cigar. He grinned, put the cigar in his mouth, and walked over to where the newsmen awaited him.

"Do you have any reactions to the election returns, Governor?"

Governor Alfred E. Smith rolled the cigar around in his mouth as if he were thinking. Then he took it out and smiled again.

"Looks kinda one-sided, doesn't it?" he replied. His voice had that familiar New York twang that sounded so strange to people in the Midwest and South.

"Are you conceding victory to Hoover?" one reporter asked.

"Not yet. Not yet," said Smith. But his voice lacked conviction.

"Where are you going now?"

"Back to the Biltmore Hotel," he said with another smile. "My family's waiting for me. This is the kind of day you should spend with your family."

"Governor Smith," said another reporter, "what do you think was the cause of the voter reaction today? Do you think they voted against your political platform, or do you think they voted against you because you are a Catholic?"

The room became still. Smith took a puff from his cigar and blew the smoke over their heads. He was thinking of his answer.

"I can only assume," he said at last, "that a lot of people liked Herbert Hoover. But," and he paused again, looking into their faces, "it seems like a lot of people had their minds made up about me. Maybe they weren't ready for a Catholic president."

"What about the hate campaign directed against you and your Church?"

"What about it?" Smith answered back.

"Do you think it affected the election?"

"Of course it affected the election," Smith said. "Good heavens! People were saying I'd bring the Pope over to run the country if I were elected. That I'd make all the Protestant kids go to parochial schools. That I'd turn the Democratic Party into a Catholic party. Those are all lies—and what's worse, they're stupid lies.

"Anyone who knows my record as governor of New York realizes that I support the Constitution of the United States, the public school system, and the absolute separation of church and state."

"How does this make you feel, Governor?" the reporter asked him again. "Are you bitter?"

The defeated candidate looked at the reporters scribbing on their notepads. "No," he said, "I'm not bitter. I've been in politics for 33 years—as governor, legislator, and alderman. A politician learns not to make enemies and to take the good with the bad."

A young newsman thrust himself forward from the crowd. "Assuming that the present trend in the election continues and that you lose—what will you do then?"

A slow grin spread across the governor's face.

"I don't know," he said. "Maybe I'll go back to selling fish!"

And with the reporters' laughter following him, the defeated candidate tugged on his hat brim and stepped out into the chilly November night.

When a woman once asked Al Smith whether he ever graduated from college, he smile, bowed, and responded: "Madam, I hold the degree of F.F.M.—Fulton Fish Market."

It wasn't just a joke. At the age of nineteen young Alfred Smith worked at the market on Manhattan's teeming lower East Side. Getting to work at 4 a.m. (3 a.m. on Fridays), he hoisted crates, cleaned and sold fish, and stood on the roof with a spyglass to watch for fishing boats coming in. It was an exhausting, dirty, and smelly job. He earned $12 a week.

The money was considered good in 1892. It was sorely needed in the Smith household where Al provided most of the money to support his mother and younger sister. His father had died six years earlier.

New York in those days was a cauldron of races, religions, and nationalities. It was a port of entry for most of the immigrants arriving from Europe. The Jews from eastern Europe were pouring into the United States in great numbers, and the first waves of Italian immigrants were just appearing.

Deprived of higher education and a chance of advancement in the professional fields, these new Americans found politics to be one area where they could advance themselves and their people. Local political clubs got jobs for them, provided food when they were hungry, gave them cash when they were broke, and sometimes got them out of jail when they had a scrap. The parish church and the political club were the welfare agencies of their day.

It is hardly a wonder that young Al Smith stepped into politics as easily as he walked into church. He was a bright boy, friendly, hard-working. From working as a delivery boy and on the docks he knew almost everyone by their first names. Also, he was a good speaker, a skill he picked up in an amateur theater group at St. James Parish.

Democratic Party leaders had noticed the quick and likable young man. After serving in some local jobs, he was nominated in 1903 to run for the State Assembly, and he won.

The new legislator knew almost nothing about making laws and running the government. But then, he didn't have to. The party leaders back in the city told him how to vote. Smith was an obedient machine politician who did what he was told. That's how things worked.

But in 1911 something changed all that. A fire broke out in a New York clothing factory killing

150 young women who worked there. The victims were all immigrants or the daughters of immigrants.

Named to an investigating committee Smith discovered the appalling truth that there were no safety rules for such "sweatshop" factories. Companies could hire people of any age and compel them to work long hours for dreadfully low wages in unsafe buildings. Incensed by what he saw, Smith helped to write strong new laws that protected workers. In other areas, too, he discovered that the government wasn't serving the poor and needy—his own kind of people— as it should.

Smith had dropped out of school before he finished the eighth grade. Now he worked long hours by himself, reading reports, studying budget recommendations. He taught himself how governments work, and why they sometimes fail to work. Far from being a hack politician, he was turning himself into a "reform" politician, dedicated to the social betterment of New Yorkers.

He served twelve years in the New York State Assembly, and by the time he left he knew more about government than any man in the state. Instead of taking orders from the city bosses, he gave orders.

In 1918 he ran for governor and won. Although defeated narrowly in 1920, he was reelected in 1922, and again in 1924 and 1926. He had a solid progressive record, supporting women's rights, child welfare laws, public housing.

By 1924 there was already talk about Smith running for president. He would have been a good choice, but he was a Catholic.

No Catholic had ever been elected president. Over the years there had been two Catholic Supreme Court chief justices and some senators and cabinet members, but never had a major party nominated a Catholic for the presidency. Old anti-Catholic hatreds were just too strong.

This prejudice was reinforced in the 1920s by the reemergence of the Ku Klux Klan, a secret society of prejudiced whites who preached hatred for blacks, Jews, and other minorities, including Catholics. Born after the Civil War, the Klan had almost disappeared until it experienced a boom in membership after World War I. In 1924 the Klan numbered about five million members, all of them bitterly opposed to the idea of a Catholic president. They succeeded in swinging the Democratic nomination away from Al Smith to John W. Davis, a Wall Street lawyer.

Davis lost the election. four years later the Democratic Party could not deny Smith. Their convention nominated him for president on the first ballot.

The election of 1928 should have been a dignified campaign between two distinguished candidates: Al Smith and Herbert Hoover. It should have been, but it wasn't.

The candidates themselves behaved well, both of them touring the country in special railroad trains, making speeches at each town's station.

It wasn't Hoover's speeches, it was the whispering campaign, the nasty gossip, and the ugly prejudice that did the damage to Al Smith.

His New York accent was an object of scorn. His lack of full support for Prohibition was viewed as a sign of personal weakness. But above all his Catholicism worked against him.

Vicious circulars and cartoons suggested that the Pope would rule the country if Smith were elected. The Ku Klux Klan was making one last effort to deny the White House to a Catholic. Anti-Catholic feelings ran so high that in Louisville Smith had to be escorted by a squad of special police through an angry crowd.

Some of the opposition came from respected quarters. The *Christian Index,* a Protestant publication in Georgia, declared: "Put Alfred E. Smith's church in power and out goes the people's democratic Constitution, and with it goes popular representative government...free thought, free press, free worship; in come the ecclesiastical courts and the canon liquor traffic at high tide—because Rum, Romanism, and Rebellion form law..."

In Oklahoma City Smith tried to answer the hate campaign. He called it an attempt "to inject bigotry, hatred, intolerance, and un-American sectarian division into a campaign which should be an intelligent debate of the important issues which confront the American people."

It was no use. Anti-Catholic feelings were too deep. As a Baptist minister in Birmingham declared openly, "I am against Smith and so is every other Baptist—and one of every three men in Alabama is a Baptist."

In November Hoover won the election by polling 20 million votes to Smith's 14 million. Hoover won the electoral vote by 444 to 87.

In many ways the election was unfortunate for the United States. A year after Hoover was elected the nation fell into a terrible economic depression—businesses failed, millions of people were out of work. There is reason to think that Smith, with his imagination and knowledge of government, would have done better than the inept Hoover.

Al Smith didn't go back to selling fish after he lost the presidential election. He remained in New York to see Franklin Delano Roosevelt become the new governor. A year later he became chairman of the Empire State Building Corporation, helping to put up what was then the world's tallest skyscraper.

But Smith was still a politician at heart. He hoped to be nominated for the presidency in 1932. When the call went to Roosevelt instead, Smith was hurt and disappointed. The reform program that Roosevelt set in motion to get the country out of its depression was much like the one Smith had pioneered in New York.

Smith frankly wanted to be president. But he didn't really think of himself becoming a "Catholic" president. He didn't think religion mattered when it came to voting for someone, and he certainly didn't believe his religion should exclude him from public office.

"I am unable to understand how anything that I was taught to believe as a Catholic could possibly be in conflict with good citizenship," he once said. "The essence of my faith is built on the Commandments of God. The law of the land is built upon the Commandments of God. There can be no conflict between them."

Yet a large number of Americans continued to

be afraid that Catholics—if they somehow "got control" of the country—might try to impose their beliefs on other people. When President Harry Truman wanted to appoint an American ambassador to the Vatican in 1947, there was such a storm of protest that he had to drop the idea.

Attitudes changed slowly. It was not until 1960 that John F. Kennedy, a Catholic, was elected president of the United States. Even then some people worried about Kennedy's religion, but his record in the White House ended their fears. Gradually the virulent kind of anti-Catholic prejudice disappeared from American life.

By the time of Kennedy's election, however, Al Smith had been dead for fourteen years. Smith was gone, but everything that he worked for still stood—the Fulton Fish Market, the Empire State Building, the rights of immigrant workers, and, of course, the Commandments of God.

Knute Rockne
Gives Cause for Pride

Three years after Al Smith lost the presidential election, news of an accident in Kansas exploded across the nation's newspapers.

An airplane crashed into a field near Bazaar, Kansas, killing the pilot, copilot, and six passengers. Air travel was in its infancy in those days and crashes were not uncommon. Most crashes were not even widely reported. The bodies were taken to nearby Cottonwood Falls where they were examined by the county coroner. He stared hard at the body of a stocky, middle-aged man whose dead hands still gripped a rosary. The coroner's assistant, who was going through the victim's papers, suddenly said, "My God! It looks like this man is Knute Rockne!"

From that moment the airplane crash in Kansas was no longer an ordinary affair. Telegraph lines carried the news from coast to coast. People whispered to each other in amazement, "Have you heard? Rockne's dead."

A terrible sadness seemed to afflict everyone who heard the news. At 43, Rockne was too young to die. He had been a man of tremendous vitality and enthusiasm. He always seemed so full of life.

But most of all, Rockne was loved.

The funeral a few days later in South Bend, Indiana, was an outpouring of public affection to a degree America had not witnessed since Lincoln was murdered. Expressions of sorrow came from President Herbert Hoover, King Haakon of Norway where Rockne had been born, from Will Rogers, General Douglas MacArthur, and Charles Lindbergh.

The entire city of South Bend closed down on the day of the funeral. Nearly 100,000 people lined the streets to witness the funeral cortege, which is remarkable when one considers that the total population of South Bend was only 100,000. Trains and busses going through the city stopped for a minute of silence. The funeral Mass itself was carried on national radio.

Who was this man? A political leader? A movie star? A war hero? He was none of those. Knute Rockne was the head football coach at Notre Dame University. But to call Rockne "just" a coach would be like calling Everest "just" a mountain. Rockne was a monument—the very symbol of college football. In an era when Babe Ruth had transformed baseball, when Bill Tilden had changed the sport of tennis, and when Bobby Jones brought new glory and brilliance to golf, Rockne was a sports original; he made the game of football something unique.

Turn back the clock eighteen years. It is 1913. The place is not Kansas or Indiana but the Hudson River Valley of New York, resplendent in autumn foilage.

The United States Military Academy at West Point sits on top of a bluff, guarding against the possiblity of an invasion from the north. No keen-eyed sentry challenged the eighteen young men who tumbled from the Chicago train on October 31, although perhaps someone should have. The young men were football players from a small college in the Midwest called Notre Dame. Their team had been asked on short notice to fill an empty date in the West Point football schedule. No one expected the Midwest team to win. Army, after all, was one of the best teams in the East, and eastern football was the best in the United States. Notre Dame was so poor and unknown that Army had to give them $1000 to help pay for their travel.

What the Army didn't know was that the Notre Dame players had prepared a surprise for them. It was the forward pass.

Football teams had been throwing forward passes for years, of course, but not frequently. Football in 1913 was a running game. The ball in those days was too fat to throw easily, and receivers hadn't learned the art of catching it on the run.

But Notre Dame had been practicing that very thing. Their quarterback was Gus Dorais and their pass-catching end was a former postal clerk from Chicago named Knute Rockne. For months Dorais had been throwing in secret to Rockne who caught the ball in full gallop, sometimes with one hand. In their early games that year they had kept their passing skills hidden, saving them for West Point. The trap was about to be sprung.

November 1 was a typical late fall day at West Point, sunny and brisk. Midway in the first period of the game Rockne took a 25-yard pass over his shoulder and ran in for the touchdown. The Army team was aroused. Supported by their heavier, stronger line they matched the touchdown late in the period, but missed the extra point. Then, just before the end of the first half, Army did it again. The score was Army 13, Notre Dame 7.

At this point the partisan spectators in the stadium assumed that Army's superiority was beginning to tell. Notre Dame was apparently on its way to defeat.

"We felt we could win," Rockne recalled later. "But we honestly didn't think we could do it with our running game. Army was just too big and tough to move out of there. It was time to put our overhead stuff to work. We didn't think Army was quick enough or smart enough to adjust its defenses."

As it turned out, Army wasn't. With the seconds ticking away in the first half, Dorais threw a series of long passes, two of them to Rockne, putting the ball on the Army 5-yard line. A running play scored. Notre Dame led 14-13.

The second half was all Notre Dame. The West Pointers simply couldn't cope with Dorais' passing. And when they dropped their defenders back to knock down the passes, Notre Dame halfbacks ran up the middle. The final score was 35-14. Notre Dame had gained 243 yards by passing, an incredible total for that day, and Rockne had been a key receiver.

The next day the *New York Times* could hardly contain its excitement: "The Westerners flashed the most sensational football that has been seen in the East this year, baffling the cadets with a style of open play and a perfectly developed forward pass which carried the victors down the field at thirty yards a clip…Football men marvelled at this startling display of open football."

Two days later when the team returned to Indiana the entire student body and all the priests on the faculty met the players at the station with cheers and fireworks.

A legend was being born.

If the Notre Dame football team was becoming legendary, Rockne was the one who made it that way.

A year after the Army game he graduated as a student and was hired as an assistant football coach. He also took on the job of teaching chemistry. In fact he could have become a distinguished chemist working with Father Julius Nieuwland, who later became famous as one of the developers of synthetic rubber.

For four years Rockne worked in the classroom and on the football field. Then, in 1930, he became head coach and decided to devote his attention to football.

For the next thirteen years Rockne was the head coach at Notre Dame, and by the time of his death that small, Catholic college in Indiana was the preeminent football power in the United States. Notre Dame teams coached by Rockne won 105 games, lost only 12, and tied 5. His winning percentage was better than any college coach before or since. His teams had five undefeated seasons and won three national championships.

He achieved fame not only because he won football games, but because he did it with style. Rockne's teams were faster and better drilled than their opponents. They developed new plays and formations like the Notre Dame shift and the box formation. Some people called him a magician, but Rockne denied it. "The best thing I ever learned in life was that things have to be worked for," he said. "A lot of people seem to think there is some sort of magic in making a winning football team. There isn't, but there's plenty of work."

Under Rockne's leadership Notre Dame was not just a local team—not an Indiana team or a Midwest team. It was a national team. Rockne scheduled games with colleges all around the country. Soon it was drawing its players from all around the country, too. Other colleges represented their states or their regions; Notre Dame represented everyone.

Rockne always put on a show. To his players he delivered fiery pep talks that made them wildly eager to win. In Atlanta, Georgia, one time he announced in the locker room before the game that his son Billy was in the hospital. Tearfully he read a telegram from the boy pleading for a Notre Dame victory. All of the players knew and liked little Billy. They ran out on the field determined to win the game for his sake, and they did.

Later they found out that Billy was never sick or in the hospital. But by then it didn't seem to matter.

As a person Rockne was admired by nearly everyone. He had a big, friendly face and a lopsided grin. Celebrities, sportswriters, and politicians enjoyed his presence. People could stop him on the street to chat, because Rockne genuinely liked people and he loved to talk. Kids were in awe of him, his players adored him—even when he shouted at them and criticized them, which he did frequently. They never called him "coach"; he was always "Rock."

In the end there was something about Rockne and Notre Dame that was greater and more important than football. For millions of American Catholics in those days, Rockne generated a sense of pride.

Notre Dame in the 1920s was a symbol of the growing power of American immigrants. The stars of Rockne's teams had names like Carideo, Walsh, Stuhldreher, and Savoldi. Rockne himself was an immigrant, the son of a Norwegian tradesman who emigrated to Chicago.

There were still places in the United States where Catholics were not fully accepted in the 1920s. Consider what happened to Al Smith. And nowhere was the prejudice against Catholics stronger than in the eastern colleges where the sons of America's wealthy class attended school.

But when Notre Dame showed up on the football field wealth didn't count. Strength and skill were what counted, and courage, and determination. Those were qualities that Rockne and his teams had plenty of.

The morning after a game, millions of Catholic immigrants who were struggling to survive in this new country opened their newspapers to see if Notre Dame won. A victory gave them renewed hope that they, too, could find success and recognition in America.

Thanks to Knute Rockne, they found reason to hope each autumn with regularity.

By the time Rockne died Notre Dame was well established as a college football power. Other players and coaches came along to keep the legend alive. And in the process of cementing its reputation as a football school, Notre Dame also became a great university. Generations of Catholic and non-Catholic youths educated there went on to be leaders in their professions and their communities. This also was Rockne's heritage.

At his funeral in 1931, Father Charles O'Donnell, president of the university, described what Rockne meant to Catholics and to all Americans. "Everybody was proud of Rockne," said O'Donnell. "Everybody admired him. But far more than that, we loved him...He was a great personality with the attributes of genius."

But perhaps Lou Little, the coach at Columbia University, said it best: "He was the greatest football coach and the greatest fellow I ever knew."

Dorothy Day Starts a Newspaper

Dorothy Day met Peter Maurin for the first time on December 9, 1932. At the time it didn't seem to be an important meeting. She was just back from a trip to Washington, D.C.; he was waiting in her New York apartment when she returned.

She found him dressed in a wrinkled suit with a crooked tie, his large head topped by greying hair. He looked like a well-mannered hobo, like one of those jobless men she had seen parading the day before in front of the White House.

Peter said he wanted to talk to her, but Dorothy was tired from her long bus ride. She sent him away. The next day he was back.

They were poor, both of them. Peter had worked at odd jobs for many years. Sometimes he would dig ditches. Sometimes he would wash dishes. Sometimes he would teach French. But always, wherever he went, he would spend hours reading and talking about the problems of the world. He would talk to people in the street, to bums on park benches. No one would listen to him. His life seemed to be a failure.

Dorothy, too, had lived an aimless life as a journalist, never long in one place. She hung around with other artists and writers as poor as herself. She desperately wanted to make the world better, but the world was not getting better and Dorothy was discouraged. Recently she had begun to look at the condition of her own life. She became a

Christian, but she found no joy in it. She wasn't sure what to do next.

When he came back the next day, Peter let it be known that he didn't agree with Dorothy's kind of politics—all the marches and demonstrations and organized complaining that her crowd took part in. He handed her a note he had composed. It read:

People go to Washington
asking the Federal Government
to solve their economic problems,
while the Federal Government
was never intended
to solve men's economic problems.
Thomas Jefferson says that
the less government there is,
the better it is.
If the less government there is,
the better it is,
then the best kind of government,
is self-government.
If the best kind of government
is self-government,
then the best kind of organization
is self-organization.

Self-organization? What in the world was he talking about? Peter was willing to explain. In fact he explained copiously, endlessly, following her around her apartment while she was doing her housework, talking to her, explaining to her, talking while she did her washing, while she fed her daughter, even talking when she tried to listen to a musical program on the radio, until Dorothy had to exclaim, "Peter, for heaven's sake, the *music!*"

Slowly his message began to sink in. Dorothy, in Peter's opinion, was giving too much attention to politics and government, as if those institutions could improve society. They couldn't, in Peter's view. He wanted to return to something like the medieval monasteries where the poor were taken in without question. Governments would never do that. He wanted to see places where groups of people could live simply, talk and pray together, and serve people in the surrounding neighborhood.

Peter didn't just have ideas, he had plans.

"First we must have round-table discussions where ideas can be clarified," he said. "We must bring people together so they can talk."

"You mean so *you* can talk," said Dorothy.

Peter ignored her. "Next," he said, "we must have houses of hospitality, places for travelers and homeless people to go to. And later we will have farms outside the city."

"And where are you going to get the money to do this?" Dorothy asked him.

"In the history of the saints, capital was raised by prayer," Peter announced solemnly. "God sends you what you need when you need it."

The program was a simple and radical one that appealed to Dorothy. Christians had to love their neighbors; they had to form small communities where they could support each other and serve the poor.

There was one other step in Peter's program. He wanted to start a newspaper.

"A newspaper! How in the world are we going to do that?"

"The thing is just to start," Peter declared. "In the Catholic Church money is never necessary."

Dorothy stared at him. Either this man was crazy or he was a saint. She only knew she had never met a person before who had such revolutionary ideas, ideas that stirred her and filled her with hope. This plain-looking man was a visionary. Whether or not his visions would come true was going to depend on her.

Actually Dorothy Day was well-acquainted with newspapers. Her father had been a sports reporter in San Francisco and Chicago, and both of Dorothy's older brothers were journalists. Writing for newspapers was a family business.

Dorothy herself got a newspaper job as soon as she left college. But she wasn't a sports reporter. Since high school she had been reading about the condition of working people, about labor unions and socialism. She was influenced in part by her older brother Donald and by teachers in college. She liked to think of herself as a socialist.

Her first job was with the *Call*, a radical newspaper in New York City that so disturbed her father that she decided to leave home. Later she worked for *The Masses* and *The Liberator*, papers that were even more radical. Gradually she drifted into a life that her parents disliked. She lived in the poor section of town, made friends with artists and revolutionaries, and supported political movements for women, trade unions, and pacifists.

64

Polite young women were not supposed to do such things in those days, but Dorothy had decided she would not accept the rules of polite society.

Life was not always exciting and challenging for Dorothy. As much as she learned about the world, she also learned unhappiness in her private life. She fell in love with a man who didn't love her, and then she married another man whom she didn't love. The marriage ended in divorce. Dorothy moved to Chicago and New Orleans, working on newspapers and doing other odd jobs. She wanted to make the world better. The only thing she was doing was making her own life worse.

All her life she had been looking for some system of belief that would satisfy her idealism and give her an outlet for her energies. As a girl, she went through a religious phase, but in college she dropped all that and turned to politics. Yet she never completely lost her religious feeling. In New Orleans she used to drop into the old St. Louis Cathedral on Jackson Square for evening benediction. There was something about it that was comforting to her.

Back in New York Dorothy fell in love again, and this time gave birth to a daughter. The event had a powerful effect on her. She wanted more happiness for her daughter than she herself had found. She decided she would have the child baptized.

Her decision was an odd one. Dorothy was not a Christian at this time, despite visits to churches now and then. Still, Dorothy was a person who made up her mind swiftly. She was determined to have her daughter baptized and to be baptized herself—for how could she raise a Christian daughter if she was not one? The matter was rapidly arranged. After a few months of instruction by a nun in Staten Island, N.Y., Dorothy was received into the Catholic Church in 1927.

Dorothy was in the Church, yes, but what was she going to do there? None of her fellow Catholics knew what to make of this radical newspaperwoman who came to their churches to pray. And nearly all of her old friends—atheists, most of them—were embarrassed by her conversion and stayed away from her. It seemed that by finding God Dorothy had lost almost everyone else.

She wrote some articles for Catholic magazines like *Commonweal*. She earned a few dollars; not much, but Dorothy never wanted to be wealthy. She had been on a reporting trip to Washington that night when she came back to find Peter Maurin in her apartment.

Peter was giving her a plan of action that fit in with her new-found faith. His talk about the dignity of work, his desire to live simply, gathering friends in small communities to pray and serve the poor—all these were similar to the feelings she had cherished since she was a girl. Dorothy was a doer; Peter was a dreamer. Together, perhaps, they could make something happen.

Peter's wish to start a newspaper—even though they both were poor—was a good place to start. Dorothy had been reading the story of Rose Hawthorne Lathrop who had begun a cancer hospital without any help. Dorothy would try the same kind of thing.

"If we had a mimeograph machine, we could have a mimeographed newspaper," she said. "But all we have is my typewriter."

So she started typing. A Catholic printer agreed to print 2500 copies of an eight-page paper for $57. She had just enough money to pay for it.

They decided to call it the *Catholic Worker* because the name sounded like the communist paper, the *Daily Worker*. Dorothy wanted to give copies away free, but the Post Office wouldn't give them a mailing license for a free paper. So they decided to price the paper at one penny—"to indicate how little we thought about money," said Dorothy later.

In those years May 1, or "May Day," was the usual time when union members and liberals and radicals of all kinds came together in large demonstrations to support their political and economic programs. As usual, the New York demonstration in 1933 took place at Union Square where 50,000 people crowded together.

Among the throng were Dorothy and three friends handing out copies of the first issue of the *Catholic Worker*. She had the help of a college student, Joe Bennett, and two teenagers from a nearby parish.

The tough laboring men in the crowd looked at the paper skeptically. There were rude remarks from some of the demonstrators, but Dorothy paid them no mind. Other people seemed to take the paper and read it. After a while the teenagers grew embarrassed and went home. Dorothy and Bennett remained to the end, satisfied that they were starting something that would touch many lives.

As it turned out, the little newspaper was an immediate success. Within one year they were printing 35,000 copies of each issue. Papers were being mailed to all parts of the United States and to Europe.

Readers had to pay attention to the *Catholic Worker* because Dorothy Day and her friends actually did what they talked about—they lived with the poor and cared for them. If hungry or homeless people came by, they were given food and clothes and a place to sleep.

It happened very simply, as Dorothy remembered it: "We were just sitting there when lines of people saying, 'We need bread,' began to form. We could not say, 'Go away and be filled.' If we had six small loaves and a few fishes, we had to share them. It all happened while we sat there talking, and it is still going on."

Life at the Catholic Worker House was like life in the early Church at the time of the apostles. Peter Maurin described it to his readers:

In the first centuries
of Christianity
the hungry were fed
at a personal sacrifice,
the naked were clothed
at a personal sacrifice,
the homeless were sheltered
at a personal sacrifice.
And because the poor
were fed, clothed and sheltered
at a personal sacrifice,
the pagans used to say about the Christians
"See how they love each other."

In our own day
the poor are no longer
fed, clothed and sheltered
at a personal sacrifice
but at the expense
of the taxpayers.
And...the pagans say about the
Christians
"See how they pass the buck."

Dorothy Day had started a newspaper, but she started something much more than that. The Catholic Worker Movement was a way for Christians to behave. The movement spread from city to city. Houses of hospitality were begun where needy people could be helped. Farms were started where people could learn to live simply and close to nature.

Dorothy was no longer just a newspaper writer. She became a modern apostle: teaching, helping, caring for people for nearly fifty years. She went all over the country telling people about the Catholic Worker ideal. And even after her death the work she and Peter Maurin started continues at Cathlolic Worker houses.

And, of course, the newspaper she started continues to be sold. At a penny a copy.

Thomas Merton
Is Rescued
by His Father,
More Than Once

The New York Central Railroad train charged through the night between Buffalo and Cleveland, rain and sleet slashing against its lighted windows. Inside, the passengers were just beginning to settle down for a long ride. Some of them were going home for the holidays. Christmas was not far away. A few of them had other business. In one corner were four young men who had left college that day to enlist in the Armed Forces.

It was December 8, 1941. On the previous day Japan had bombed the American naval base at Pearl Harbor. The United States was plunged suddenly into a world war. Everyone on that train—indeed, everyone in the world—faced months and years of suffering, sacrifice, and death.

In one seat by himself was a young man with close-set eyes and thinning, sandy hair gazing silently into the dark night. On that very day he, too, had left St. Bonaventure College where he taught. But he wasn't going home or to his draft board. The train was taking him on a different journey. He was going to Kentucky, where he hoped to enter a monastery and forever hide himself from the turmoil and death he saw in the world around him. He wished to be a man of peace at a moment when everyone else seemed eager for war. But to do so, he knew, he would have to die to his old life, to all the people and places he knew. He would have to put them all behind him.

He stared out the window and tried to decipher the rhythm of the wheels. They seemed to say, "Nowhere. Nowhere...."

He was only twenty-six but he had spent a good part of his life on trains and boats, traveling. He never had a real home. Born in New York, he lived much of his early life in France and England. Always, it seemed, he was off to some new place with his father, an artist who painted pictures. He lived in boarding schools or stayed with friends of his parents. He never stayed in one place long. First his mother died, and then his father. He lived for a time with relatives. He spent his days aimlessly roaming through the streets of cities—browsing in bookstores, going to movies, drinking too much, wasting his time.

His relatives would shake their heads sadly. Tom was such a nice boy. But he was throwing his life away.

He was a person without roots. Yet, as he moved through the cities of his youth, his eyes were filled with compassion for the suffering people he saw around him. Living one summer among the tenements of Harlem he saw how "souls are destroyed by vice and misery and degradation, obliterated, wiped out, washed from the register of the living, dehumanized." He saw them and he suffered with them.

He had a capacity for deep feeling. He remembered the time in Rome when he was admiring the beautiful art of churches. He wandered alone into the Church of Saints Cosmos and Damian when he was suddenly confronted by the huge mosaic of Christ above the altar. The young man who never prayed, who claimed to be an atheist, stood there in a kind of shock. Here was an experience he had never had before: It was God.

But the moment passed. He returned to his travels and forgot all about it. As a student at Cambridge University he fell into new kinds of experiences. Studying, unfortunately, was not one of them. Instead he wasted his time on drunkenness and sensuality, late hours, parties, extravagant spending, and at the end of it all…sadness.

He was sent back to New York in disgrace to live with his grandparents. When they died, one by one, he wept and tried to pray at their bedsides. Then he packed up again and moved into an apartment. Alone. Homeless.

Poor, lonely Thomas Merton. He had lived more in his twenty-six years than most people lived in a full lifetime. His own suffering had given him a good measure of compassion for other people in pain. Looking out the train window he tried to imagine the people who lived in the little Ohio villages. He understood that they were lonely sometimes, even those who had homes. He understood by this time that loneliness is a place where we come close to God and discover who we truly are.

"For each of us," he once wrote, "there is a point of nowhereness in the middle of movement, a point of nothingness in the middle of being…If you seek it, you will not find it. If you stop seeking it, it is there."

Now at last he was able to pray, for himself, for everyone.

The train wheels spoke, "Nowhere. Nowhere…" He was going home.

Six years before that fateful train ride, Thomas Merton had been an undergraduate student at Columbia University, still living with his grandparents in Queens, riding the train every day to school, looking at the faces on the train and being moved by the toil and hopelessness he saw in people around him.

Ever since he was a boy he had felt there was something wrong with a world that caused so much suffering. So many people felt trapped in their jobs, in their neighborhoods, and by an economic system that kept them in chains. Merton believed passionately that the system needed to be changed. He had read Karl Marx as a schoolboy and was convinced that communism was the answer to human suffering. In the 1930s, with a great depression gripping the United States and the world, it was easy to be a communist.

Like Dorothy Day, Merton eagerly joined the great communist adventure to make society better, once and for all. He took part in demonstrations, signed petitions, did everything that polite college students do in their tentative efforts to change the world.

But even as he did these things, Merton was suspicious of them. He felt there was an element of play-acting in the student activities. Some of his fellow students talked about violent revolution, but it was apparent that these sons and daughters of wealthy parents would never rebel against a society that was constructed for their comfort and prosperity.

At one communist group meeting Merton was given the code name "Frank Swift." There was a lot of talk about the need for secrecy. Merton thought the whole thing was funny.

There was nothing funny, however, about the real pain and suffering the world was going through in the 1930s. People everywhere were without jobs. In Italy and Germany Fascist dictators were preaching racial hatred and violence. The Japanese warlords were brutalizing China. Everywhere one looked there was fear and oppression. In Merton's opinion the world was like a "shipwreck." One had to flee from it or drown.

Once, when Merton was a young boy, his father had enrolled him in a French boarding school that young Thomas hated. The French boys picked on him. The school was cold and hostile. For two years Tom had begged to be taken out, to no avail. Then one day his father appeared unexpectedly and announced they were going to England to stay. Joyously Tom ran to pack his bags and go. He remembered that as the car went down the drive his mind silently exulted: "Liberty. Liberty. Liberty…."

Now in 1938 his father came for him again— not his own long-dead father, but the Father he had seen in the church in Rome, the Father who had been waiting to rescue him.

Merton had come to realize that communism was not the answer. The real revolution, he felt, needed to take place in people's hearts, and in his own heart. Slowly, shyly, he learned to pray. At last he decided he could no longer remain a fashionable atheist. He became a Catholic.

His faith gave Merton a new sense of identity and purpose. He was no longer Frank Swift. He didn't need to be an artificial person. He could be himself. For years he had felt compassion for the downtrodden. Now he understood why: he was their brother in Christ.

His conversion transformed Merton's life powerfully. The full impact was brought home to him one night while walking in New York City with him friend Robert Lax. Casually Lax asked him, "Who do you want to be, anyway?"

Merton said he wanted to be a good Catholic.

"What you should say," Lax replied, "is that you want to be a saint."

"How do you expect me to become a saint?"

"By wanting to."

Merton was perplexed. "I can't be a saint!" Sanctity seemed like an impossible goal.

"All that is necessary to be a saint is to want to be one," Lax answered. "Don't you believe that God will make you what he created you to be if you will consent to let him do it? All you have to do is desire it."

Merton did desire it. He decided to become a priest. When his plans to enter the Franciscan Order went awry, he turned to the Trappists instead.

"This is the center of America," he reported while visiting the Trappist monastery in Kentucky early in 1941. "I wondered what was holding the country together, what was keeping the universe from cracking to pieces and falling apart. It is places like this monastery."

He returned to New York and St. Bonaventure's where he was teaching, but his mind was made up. He would enter the monastery. He would live in silence, pray always, and be a man of peace. As the world tumbled into bloody war, Merton made one last train ride to Kentucky. The train wheels spoke the word he had heard as a boy: "Liberty. Liberty. Liberty...."

Nothing in life works out exactly as planned. That was the case with Thomas Merton, too. He thought he would live his life as a humble monk hidden away from the world.

In one way, he did. In another, he didn't.

Several years after entering the monastery, he wrote a book called *The Seven Storey Mountain* that told the story of his early years. The book became a great success, and the man who chose to lead a hidden life in a monastery was suddenly world famous.

As the years went on he produced other books— poetry, diaries, histories, instructions on prayer, and books on racial justice, war and peace, nuclear disarmament. He had not lost his compassion for suffering humankind. Indeed, the longer he spent in the monastery, the more he discovered that no person can truly hide from the world. His earlier disenchantment with modern society softened. Secure now in a home of his own with a Father who loved him, he looked upon other people with a warm and generous eye. He was given charge of the younger monks, and they referred to him fondly as "Uncle Louie."

Louie? Yes, when men enter monasteries they are given new names to symbolize the fact that they are leading new lives. Thomas Merton became Father Louis. To his reading public he was still Thomas Merton. To fellow monks he was "Louie." No one knew him anymore as Frank Swift, but the youthful compassion that made him turn briefly toward communism never left him.

In 1968 he attended a conference of monks in Bangkok, Thailand. During the conference, Merton talked about the similarities between communists and monks. Both of them, he said, are "outsiders" who refuse to go along with the world.

"In other words," he said, "the monk is somebody who says in one way or another that the claims of the world are fraudulent. What he desires is change. This puts the monk on the same plane as the Marxist."

After the talk Merton returned alone to his room in the conference center. He took a shower and in his bedroom reached up to adjust a large floor fan which, unknown to anyone, had a defective wire in it. He died, probably instantly, of electric shock.

His Father had come to take him home one last time.

Mary Lou Williams Faces the Terror of the Night

The place is Paris, France, in 1953. Walking down a busy street on the Left Bank of the city, you come across a small nightclub with its door open to passersby. A jazz piano plays inside, its sinewy music rising and falling, moving through the evening air in a clean, unbroken line to the street where walkers lift their heads to catch it. The music is joyful and yet sad, simple but hard to take apart. It seems to speak of something dark and beautiful about life.

In front of the nightclub is a poster showing a picture of the pianist, a black woman with satin smooth skin and high cheekbones. "Mary Lou Williams," the poster announces, with some other words in French. She is an American. That's not unusual. Many black Americans are living in France in the 1950s. They find less racial prejudice here than in the United States. Life is easier, opportunities are greater. And the French people love jazz.

Inside the nightclub people are crowded together to hear the American pianist. They sit with half-filled glasses and half-smoked cigarettes in their hands, listening intently as the music swirls around them. She plays a medley of songs that she wrote—"Foggy Bottom," " Pretty Eyed Baby," and "In the Land of Oo-Bla-Dee."

Finally she comes to the end of the medley. As the people in the room applaud and cheer, Mary Lou Williams doesn't seem to hear them. She glances over at the club manager and shakes her head sadly.

"What's the matter, Mary Lou?" he asks when she steps down.

"I can't do it anymore," she says.

"What do you mean you can't do it anymore? The music is wonderful! They love it."

"I don't know," she answers. She seems depressed. "I just can't play. I can't go on anymore."

"Take a break," he says gently. "You'll be fine in twenty minutes. You can lie down in my office."

"That's not what I mean," she says. "I'm quitting. For good. It doesn't mean anything to me anymore. You'll have to get someone to take my place." She looks at him sadly. "I'm sorry," she adds.

She gets her purse and coat and walks out of the club. At forty-three Mary Lou Williams has turned her back on her music. Her brilliant career is finished. Over. Done with. Ended.

It takes years of training to be a good jazz musician, but even more than that it takes instinct, a natural "feel" that you either have or don't have. Mary Lou Williams had it. It was there when she was hardly more than an infant, sitting on her mother's knee in front of the family piano back home in Atlanta. Her mother, who played the organ at the local Bapist church, would press a key and Mary Lou would imitate her. They would play together that way, sometimes they would sing. By the time she was three, she was playing by herself. She grew up with "perfect pitch," the ability to identify a note by name without looking to see which key was pressed.

When Mary Lou was five they moved to Pittsburgh. It was a happy family, but there was no father in the house and little money. By the time she was eight, Mary Lou was playing the piano at the homes of friends and relatives for whatever money she could get. Sometimes she'd come home with $20 or $30 wrapped in a handkerchief. When she was thirteen she left school for good and got a full-time job playing piano with a vaudeville group called "The Hottentots."

A musician's life isn't easy. There's a lot of traveling to do; the hours are long and late; and sometimes the jobs are few. Mary Lou Williams was a teenager traveling with grown men. Although young, she had a sense of her own dignity; the men respected and protected her.

When she was twenty, Mary Lou was playing with Andy Kirk's band out of Kansas City. This was one of the best jazz groups in the Midwest, and for the first time Mary Lou began to travel widely and to meet new people and new musicians. It was a period of great happiness.

"My, what a band that was!" she recalled later. "It was a happy band, a good-looking band, an educated band. We had a love for each other. There was a lot of love among musicians in the 1930s."

And when times were lean, they still had fun. "In Greeley, Colorado, we stayed next to a cornfield and I ate corn right up to the farmer's back door. The boys played a little semiprofessional baseball there. It was hot summertime and I carried water for them. Stumpy Brady, the trombonist, nearly got himself killed chasing balls he couldn't see. It seems you've got to starve a little before you get on."

Mary Lou Williams was getting on very well. As a teenager she had already played for such legendary jazz pianists as Fats Waller and Art Tatum. She sat in for a week with Duke Ellington's band in New York. When she wasn't actually playing, she did arranging for Kirk's band.

"I was very high-strung and sensitive," she remembered, "and when the boys fooled around at rehearsals with what I wrote I would get mad and snatch the music off the stands and begin to cry and go home to bed."

Around this time Andy Kirk's band was breaking up, so Mary Lou went to New York and began to arrange for the big bands—Benny Goodman, Cab Calloway, Glen Gray, and Tommy and Jimmy Dorsey. She did an arrangement of "Blue Skies" for Ellington and retitled it "Trumpets No End." She was also writing her own songs: "Roll 'Em," "What's Your Story, Morning Glory?" "Lonely Moments," "Whistle," "Walkin' and Swingin'," and others that became jazz classics.

As her fame began to increase in the world of jazz, her New York apartment became a meeting place for serious jazz musicians. Mary Lou Williams became a friend and helper to a whole generation of artists.

"I'd leave the door open for them if I was out," she recalled later. "Tadd Dameron would come in to write when he was out of inspiration and Thelonious Monk did several of his pieces there. Bud Powell's brother Richie learned how to improvise at my house. And everybody came or called for advice. Charlie Parker would ask what did I think about him putting a group with strings together? Or Miles Davis would ask about his group with tuba."

Mary Lou Williams by this time was a serious composer in her own right. She performed her "Zodiac Suite" at a Town Hall concert in 1945, and the next year it was performed by the New York Philharmonic Symphony Orchestra.

Despite all of her success, there were things going wrong in her life, things that she was only coming to realize. Two marriages had broken up, and the constant demands of being in the spotlight began to erode her strength.

She thought she could find peace of mind in Europe, so she scheduled a series of playing dates there. "I played in England for eleven months, and I spent money as fast as I made it," she said. She was deeply troubled by the "greed, selfishness and envy" she detected in other people and in herself.

One night at a party in England she met an American G.I. who sensed that something was wrong with her. When she told him how depressed she had become, he told her to go home and read Psalm 91. And so she did.

You will not fear the terror of the night
nor the arrow that flies by day,
Nor the plague that prowls in the darkness
nor the scourge that lays waste at noon.

Here was an answer to the nameless dread she had been feeling. Eagerly she read all the Psalms, read them over and over. They spoke with a kind of music she had never head before and with a depth of peace her own music had never achieved. She tried to continue her European tour, but the music of the Psalms—the private voice of God speaking directly to her—drowned out all other kinds of music. Her attempts to play ended finally in the Paris nightclub.

"I got a sign that everybody should pray every day," she said later. "I had never felt a conscious desire to get close to God. But it seemed that night that it all came to a head. I couldn't take it any longer. So I just left—the piano, the money, all of it."

A hundred years earlier there was an English poet named Gerard Manley Hopkins who had an experience like that of Mary Lou Williams. Hopkins made his own kind of music—the music of words. Convinced that God was calling him to a special life, he took all the poems he had ever written and burned them. He decided never to write poetry again. Many years later, after Hopkins had become a priest, he changed his mind. Today Hopkins is honored as one of the great poets in the English language.

The same kind of thing happened to Mary Lou Williams. But it took time.

After the episode in Paris, she was invited by a French musician to stay at his grandmother's house in the country to rest. "I stayed there six months, and I just slept and ate and read the Psalms and prayed," she said.

She came back to the United States determined never to play the piano again. What she wanted to do was pray and lead a holier, more disciplined life. She joined a Baptist church in Harlem, close to where she lived. But the Baptist church was closed weekdays, and Mary Lou wanted to pray every day. So she found herself going to Our Lady of Lourdes Catholic Church nearby, there to sit quietly and "meditate."

"All sorts of people came in," she remembered. "Needy ones and cripples—and I brought them home and gave them food and talked to them and gave them money. Music had left my head, and I hardly remembered playing."

As time passed she grew closer and closer to the church she visited on weekdays. Together with Lorraine Gillespie, the wife of jazz trumpeter Dizzy Gillespie, she decided to take instructions in the Catholic faith. They were received into the Church in 1957.

For some people a step like that might have been the final chapter of a story, but for Mary Lou Williams it was a new beginning. With her religious questions settled at last, she began to look around for ways to be of service with her new-found faith. Of course she could continue to bring needy people home with her. That was fine, but was it enough? She wanted to do something big.

She brought her problem to Father Anthony Woods, who had instructed her. They talked awhile, and then Father Woods said, "Mary, you're an artist. You belong at the piano. You should be writing music. My business is to help people through the Church and yours is to help people through music."

Music again? Well, she reasoned, some people had been asking her to play. Perhaps it was time.

In August of 1957 she accepted an invitation to play at a New York nightclub, the Hickory House. She was apprehensive about starting again, but it seemed to be the will of God.

"The night before I opened at the Hickory House," she said, "I had a dream. It was filled with dead musicians, all friends of mine, come back to life. Oscar Pettiford was in it, and Pha Terrell, and Dick Wilson from Kirk's band. They were all rejoicing on this kind of stage. And there was a line of showgirls dancing and singing. Oscar was very happy because I was coming out again. It was a good sign."

May Lou Williams played the piano and wrote music for another twenty years, bringing joy and inspiration to untold thousands of people. She played at the Embers, at the Town, the Cookery, and other New York music spots. She also appeared by herself and with groups at Philharmonic Hall in New York's Lincoln Center for the Performing Arts. She had her own Saturday night radio show on ABC where she introduced many listeners to the wonders of jazz.

She wrote music, too. Most of her compositions during this period had religious themes, including a hymn for St. Martin de Porres. She wrote three jazz masses. One of them became the first jazz mass ever performed at St. Patrick's Cathedral, in 1975.

Mary Lou Williams never apologized for the years she spent away from music. She explained, "There's a period when you have to stop and take care of yourself. That's the only way you can help others."

And she did continue to help others. Just as she opened her home to musicians in the 1940s and to the needy in the 1950s, she continued to offer comfort and solace to people in want. In the 1960s she founded the Bel Canto Foundation to rehabilitate musicians who suffered from alcoholism and drug addiction. To raise money for the foundation, she gave concerts and opened a second-hand clothing store in Manhattan.

In her last years new honors came to Mary Lou Williams. In 1977 she was named artist in residence at Duke Unviersity in North Carolina. *The New York Times* hailed her as "the first woman to be ranked with the greatest of jazz musicians."

Mary Lou Williams certainly appreciated that, but it didn't matter so much anymore. After facing the "terror of the night" in her own soul and finding reassurance in God, she didn't need *The New York Times* to tell her she was important.

Bibliography

Brondfield, Jerry, *Rockne: The Coach, The Man, The Legend.* New York: Random House, 1976.

Browne, Henry C., *The Catholic Church and the Knights of Labor.* Washington, D.C.: The Catholic University of America Press, 1949.

Burton, Katherine, *Sorrow Built a Bridge.* New York: Longmans Green, 1937.

Cornell, Thomas C. and Forest, James H., *A Penny a Copy: Readings from the Catholic Worker.* New York: Macmillan, 1968.

Ellis, Marc H., *Peter Maurin: Prophet in the Twentieth Century.* New York: Paulist Press, 1981.

Forest, James H., *Thomas Merton: A Pictorial Biography.* New York: Paulist Press, 1980.

Furlong, Monica, *Merton: A Biography.* San Francisco: Harper & Row, 1980.

Horgan, Paul, *Lamy of Santa Fe.* New York: Farrar, Straus & Giroux, 1980.

Lens, Sidney, *The Labor Wars.* Garden City, N.Y.: Doubleday, 1973.

Madison, Charles A., *American Labor Leaders.* New York: Frederick Ungar Publishing Co., 1950.

Merton, Thomas, *Contemplation in a World of Action,* Garden City, N.Y.: Doubleday, 1971.

--------------------, *New Seeds of Contemplation,* New York: New Directions, 1962.

--------------------, *The Seven Storey Montain,* New York: Harcourt Brace, 1947.

Miller, William D., *Dorothy Day: A Biography,* San Francisco: Harper & Row, 1982.

O'Connor, Richard, *Gould's Millions*. Garden City, N.Y.: Doubleday, 1962.

Powderly, Terence V., *The Path I Trod*. New York: Columbia University Press, 1940.

Selvin, David F., *Champions of Labor*. New York: Abelard-Schuman, 1967.

Shaw, Richard, *Dagger John: The Unquiet Life and Times of Archbishop John Hughes of New York*. New York: Paulist Press, 1977.

Smith, Ellen Hart, *Charles Carroll of Carrollton*. Cambridge: Harvard University Press, 1945.

Stone, Irving, *They Also Ran*. Garden City, N.Y.: Doubleday, 1943, 1966.

Stuhldreher, Harry A., *Knute Rockne: Man Builder*. New York: Grosset & Dunlap, 1931.

Twomey, Gerald, *Thomas Merton: Prophet in the Belly of a Paradox*. New York: Paulist Press, 1978.

Warner, Emily Smith, with Hawthorne Daniel, *The Happy Warrior*. Garden City, N.Y.: Doubleday, 1956.

GENERAL WORKS CONSULTED

The Dictionary of American Biography, X Vols. with supplements, New York: Charles Scribner's Sons, 1936, 1964.

The New Catholic Encyclopedia, XV Vols. with supplements, New York: McGraw-Hill, 1967, 1974.

The New York Times.

The New Yorker.